GRADE 1 GEOMETRY

Fun-filled Activities

An imprint of Om Books International

Open and Closed Shapes

An **open shape** is one that has an **opening** or a **break**. A **closed shape** is one that has **no opening** to get out if you were inside the lines.

open shape

closed shape

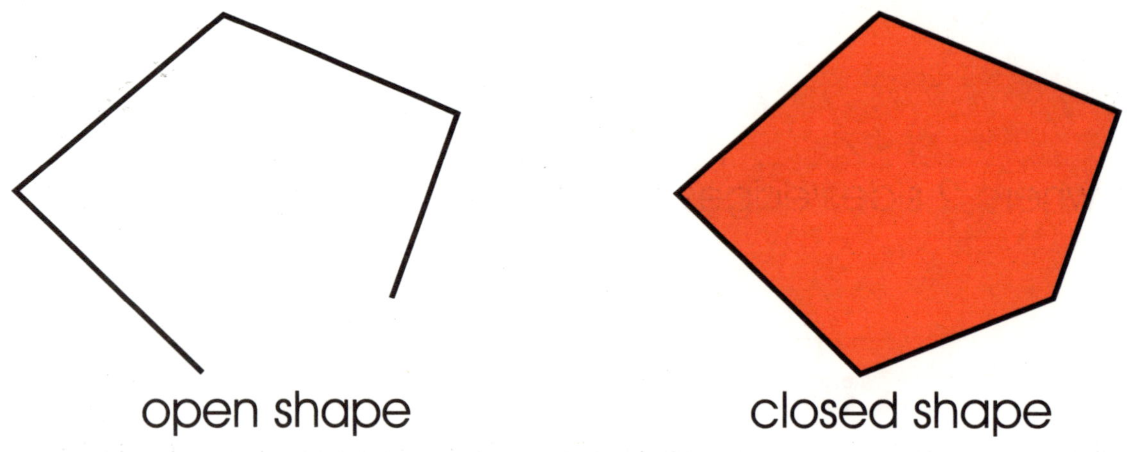

Look at the shapes. Write O for open shapes and C for closed shapes.

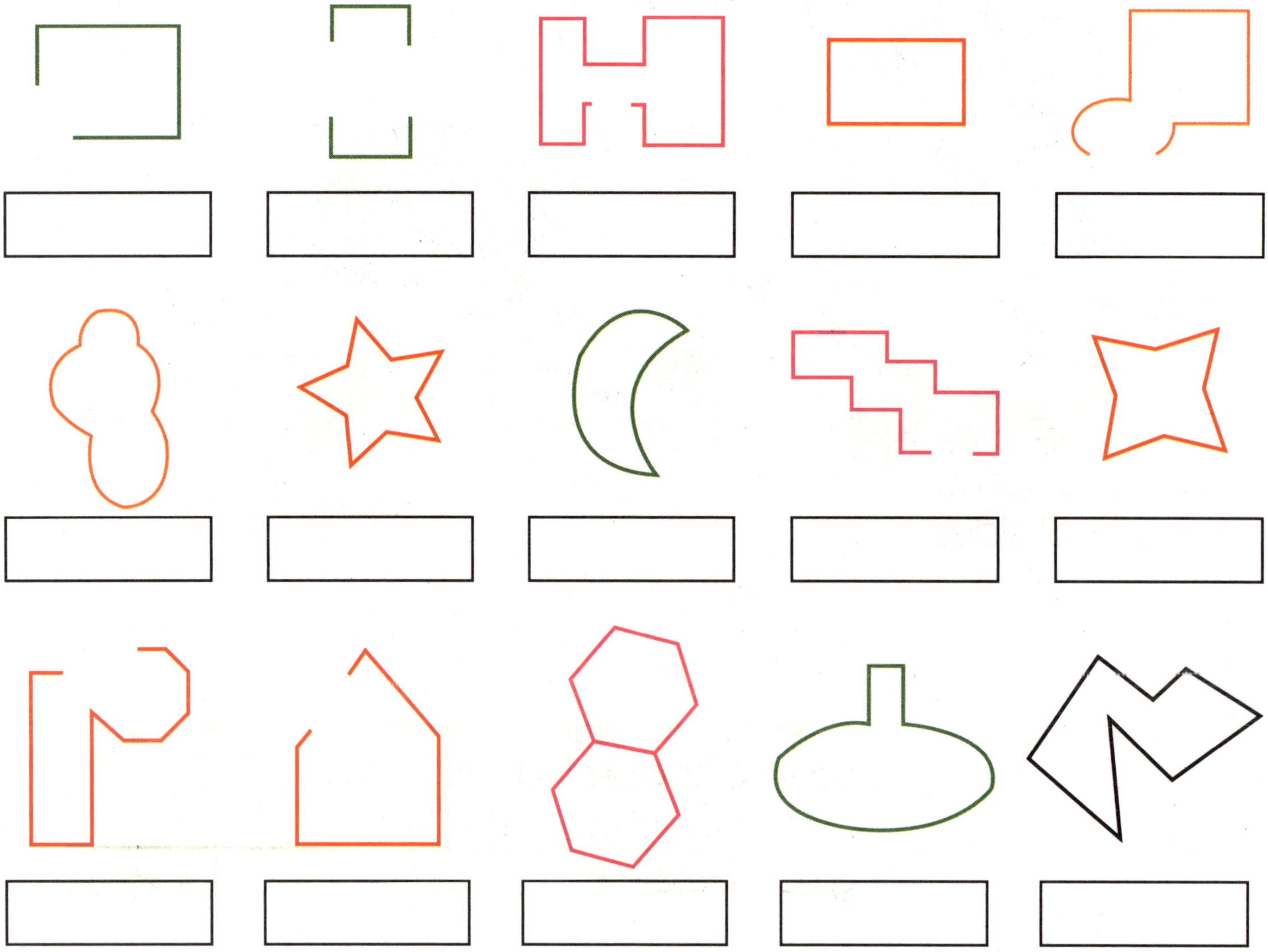

Sides and Corners

Shapes are made of line segments.

These are called **sides** or **edges.**

The point where 2 sides/edges meet is called **corner.**

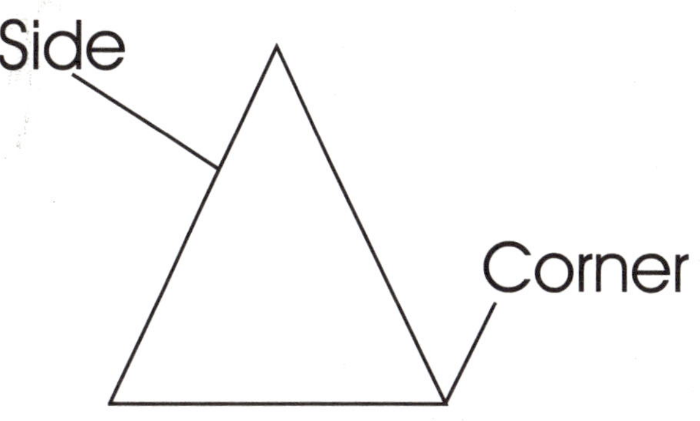

Look at these shapes and write the number of sides and corners inside each shape.

1. Colour the shape that has most number of sides.

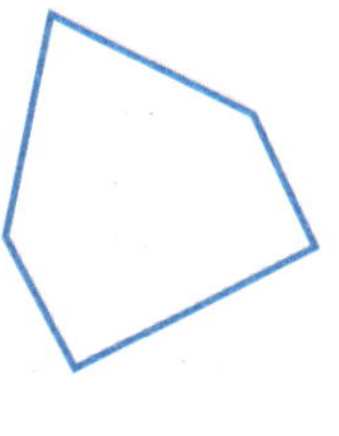 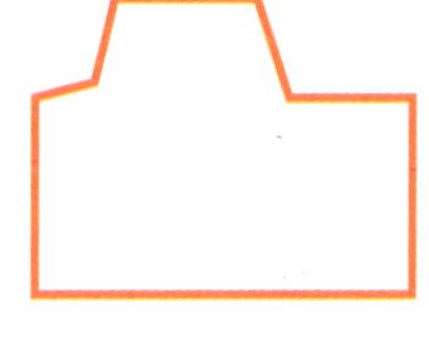 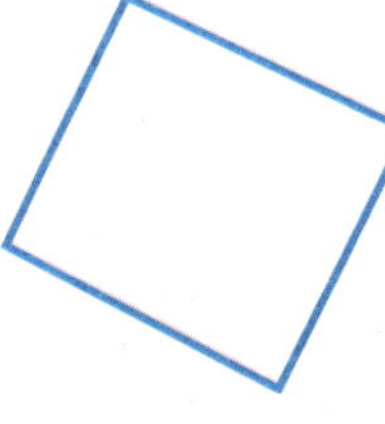

2. Tick the shape that has the least number of sides.

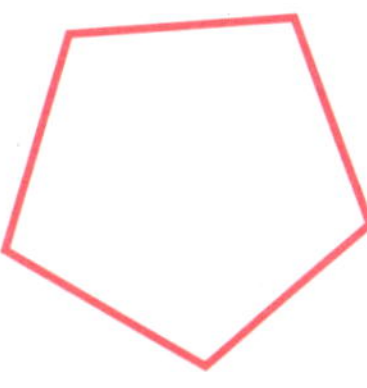 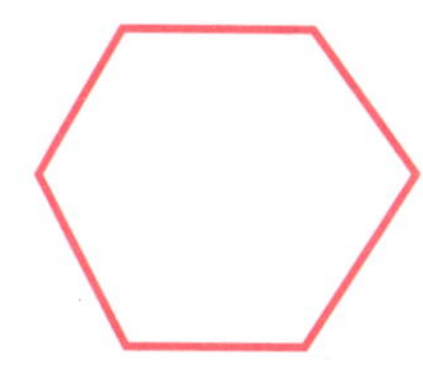 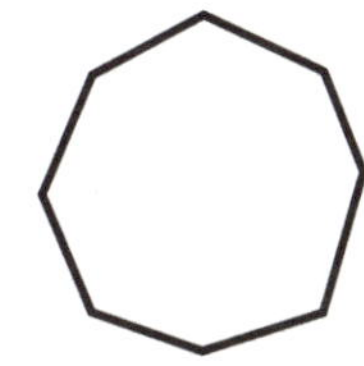

3. Match the shapes that have same number of sides.

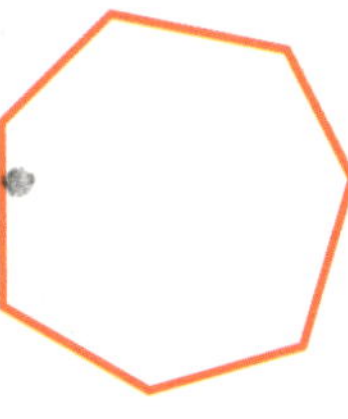 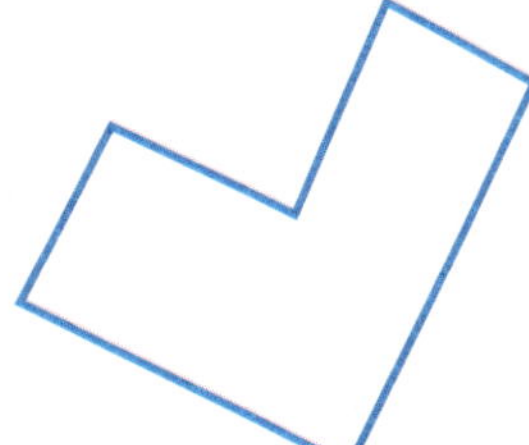 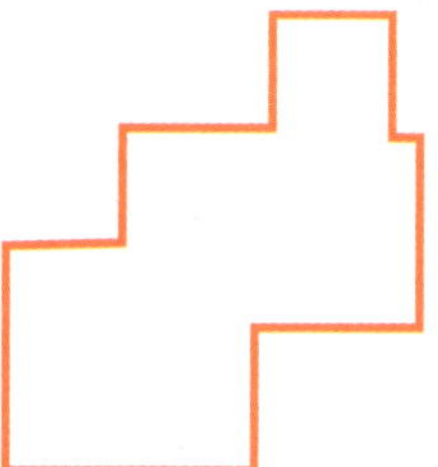

Draw a shape that has more sides than the shape given below.

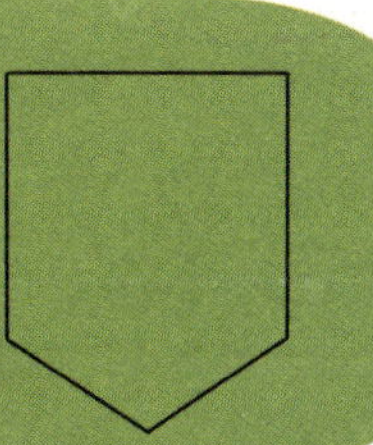

Let's Meet 2-D Shapes

Triangle

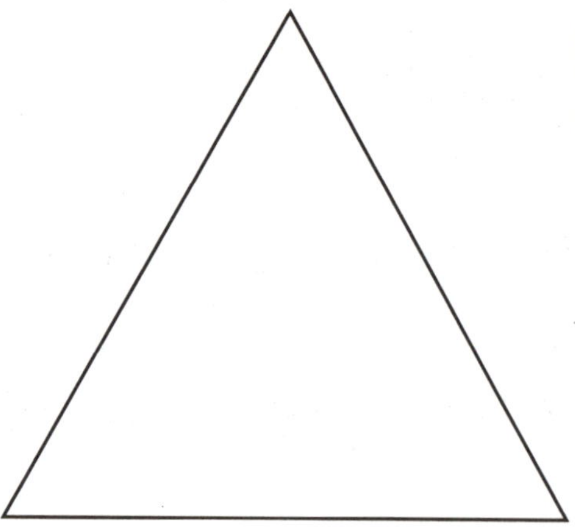

A triangle has:

- 3 sides
- 3 corners

It is a flat closed solid.

A triangle may have all sides equal or unequal.

Circle all objects that are triangular in shape.

Trace the triangles:

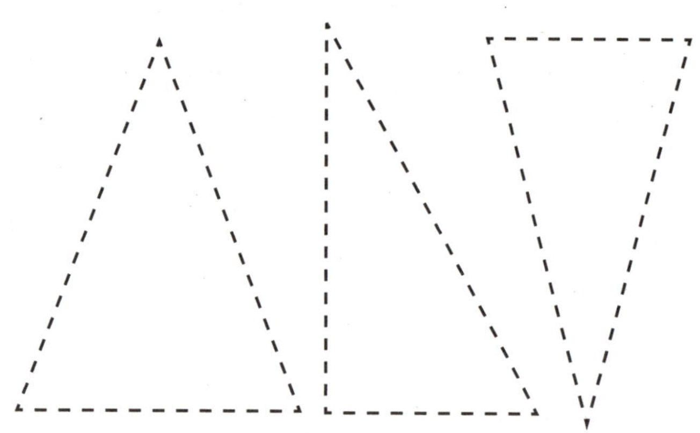

Draw a triangle

How many triangles can you see here?

Square

A square has:

- 4 sides
- 4 corners

It is a flat closed solid.

A square has all the sides and angles equal.
Its opposite sides are parallel.

A square is a special rectangle.

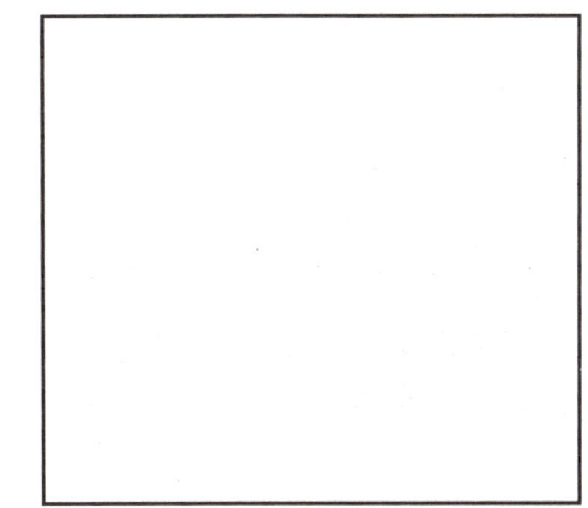

Circle all objects that are squares.

Trace the squares:

Draw a square

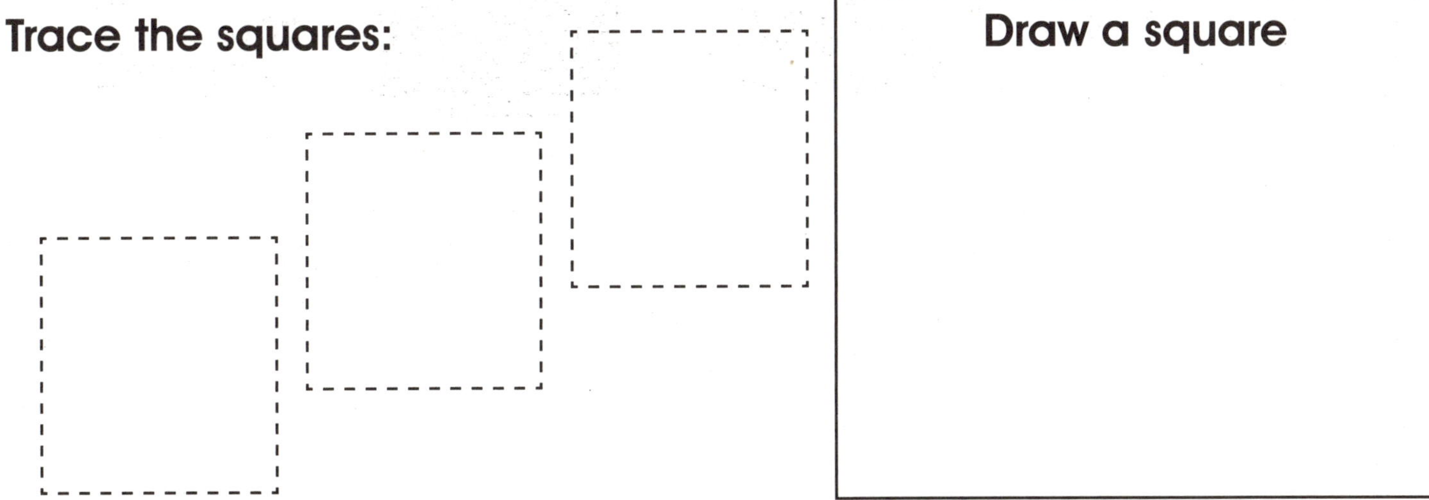

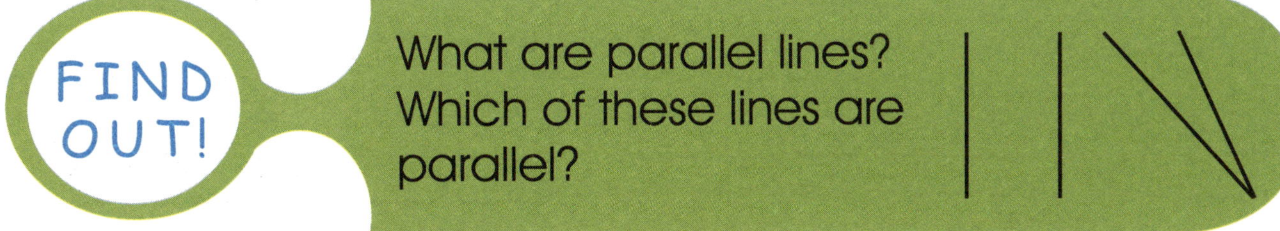

Rectangle

A rectangle has:

- 4 sides
- 4 corners

It is a flat closed solid.

A rectangle has opposite sides and equal angles.

Its opposite sides are parallel.

Tick all objects that are rectangular in shape.

Trace the rectangles:

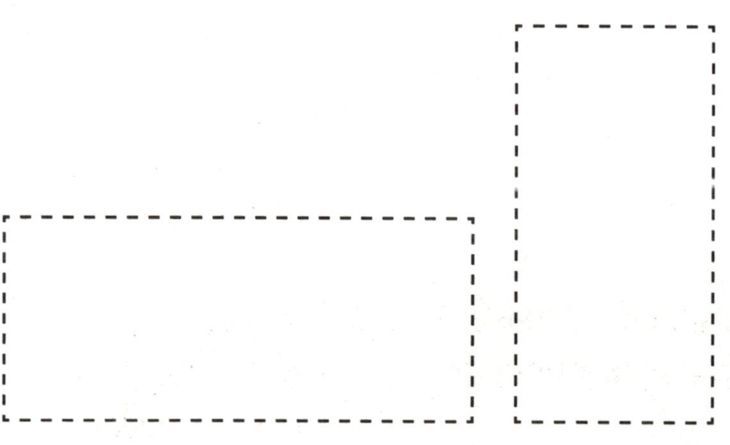

Draw a rectangle

Trapezoid

A trapezoid has:

- 4 sides
- 4 corners

It is a flat closed solid.

A trapezoid has opposite sides parallel.

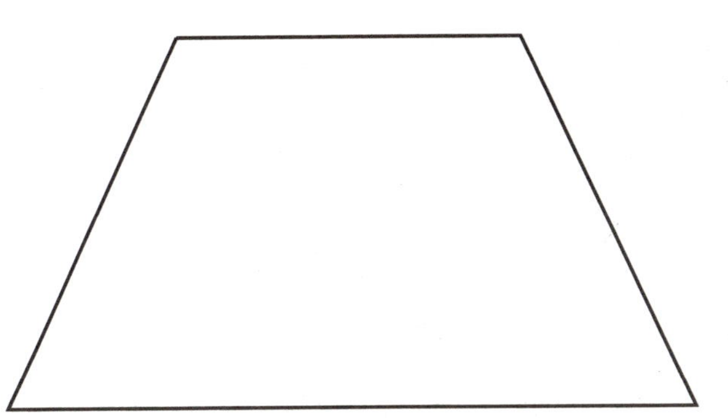

Circle all objects that are trapezoids.

Trace the trapezoids:

Draw a trapezoid

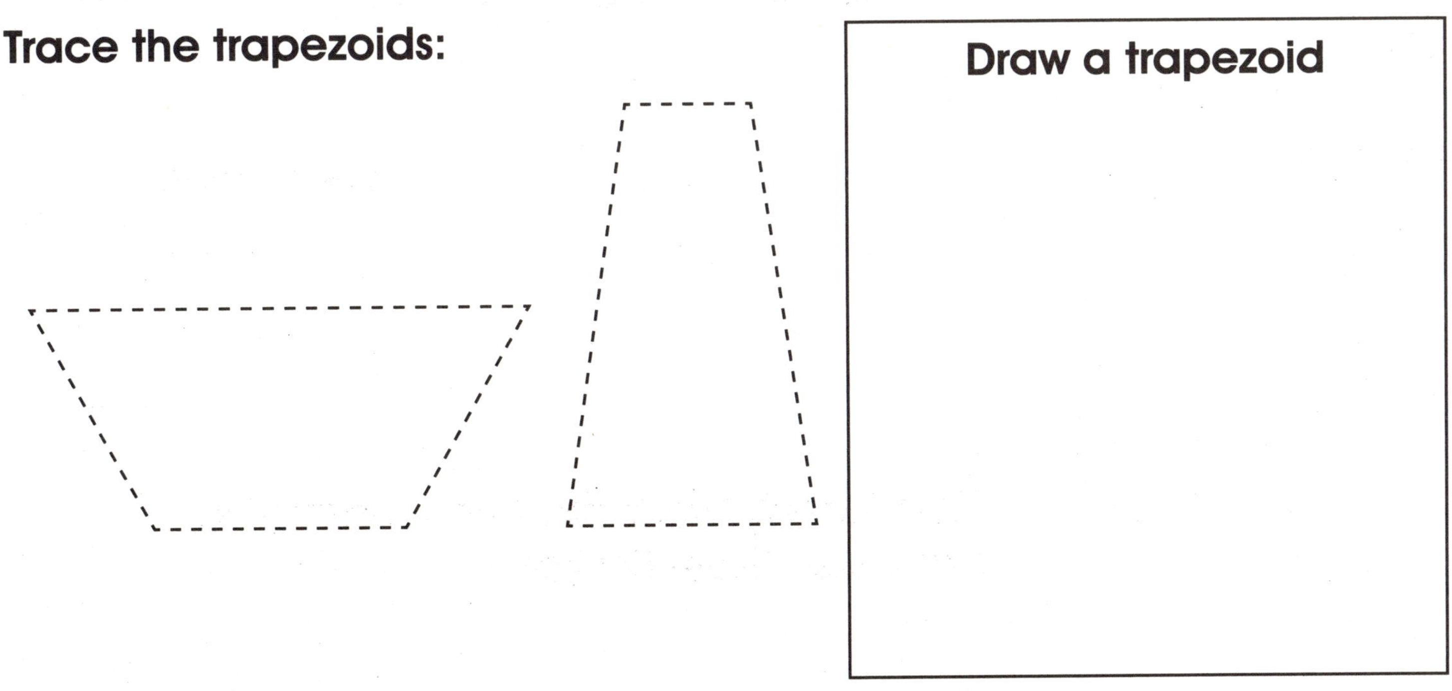

Diamond

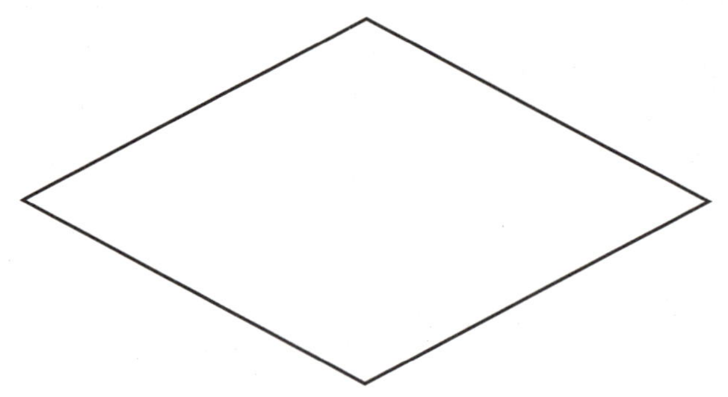

A diamond has:

- 4 sides
- 4 corners

It is a flat closed solid.

A diamond has all sides equal.

But unlike a square, a diamond doesn't have all equal angles.

Cross all objects that are diamond-shaped.

Trace the diamonds:

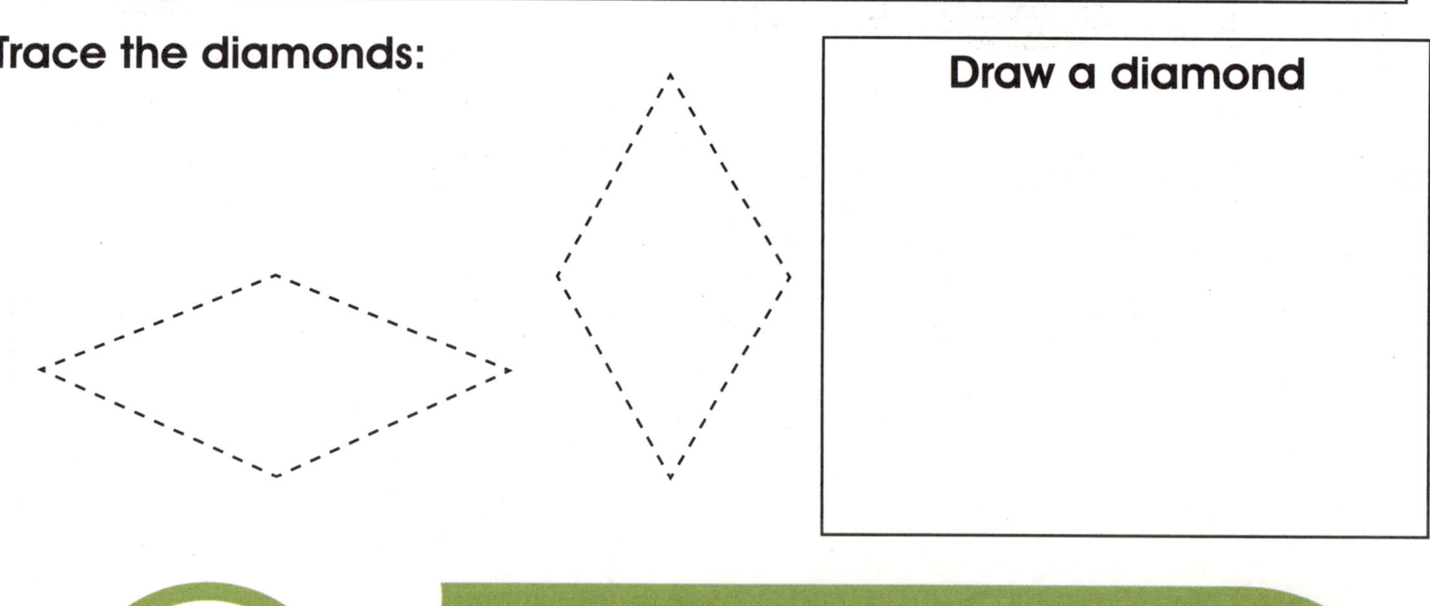

Can you make a diamond using two triangles? Give it a try!

Circle and Oval

A circle and oval have

- no sides
- no corners

These are flat closed solids.

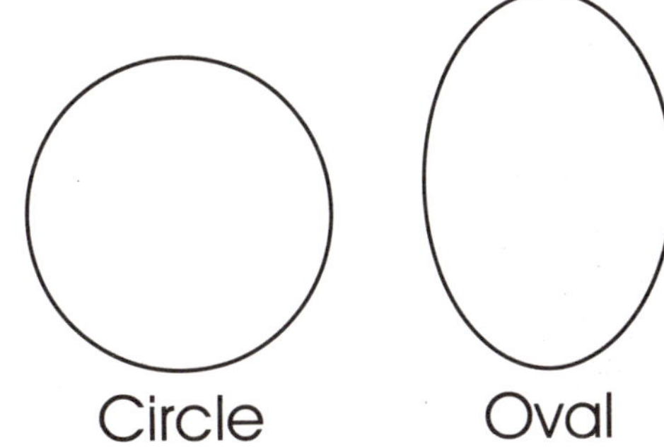

Circle all objects that are circles and cross all objects that are ovals.

Trace the circles and ovals:

Draw a circle

Draw an oval

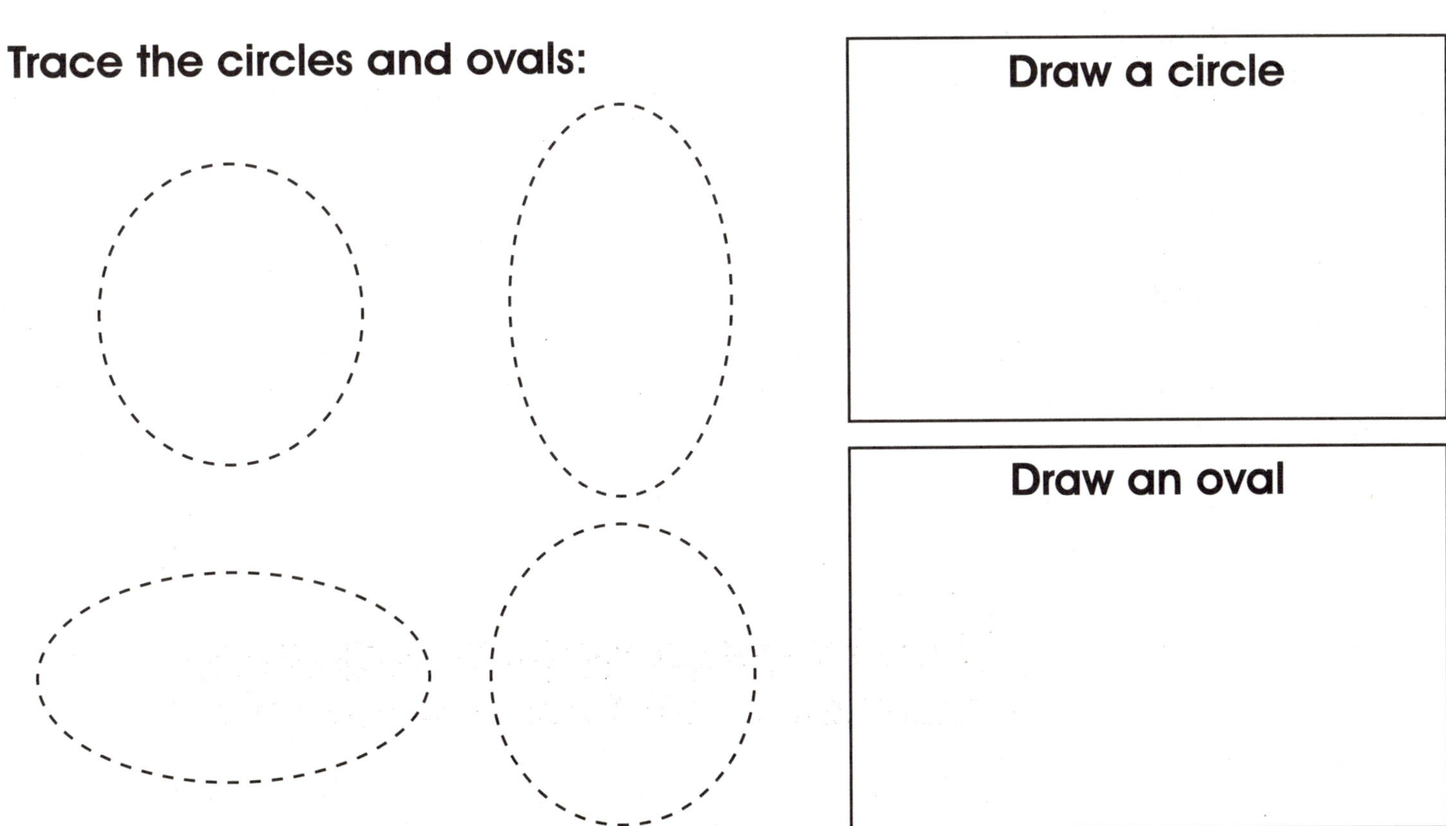

What Shape is It?

Identify and name the shape of each object. Then draw the shape.

1.	rectangle	
2.	____________	
3.	____________	
4.	____________	
5.	____________	
6.	____________	
7.	____________	

TRY IT

Draw two squares side by side joined together. Which shape do you get?

Roll and Tick the Shape

Roll a die and tick the shape or picture that matches your roll.

triangle	circle	kite	rectangle	square	trapezoid

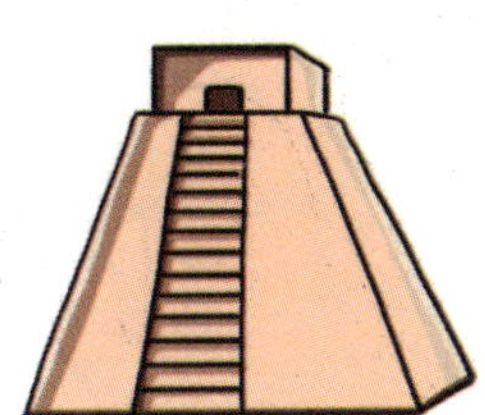

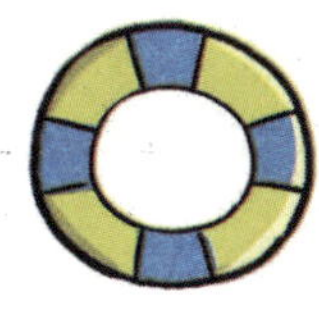

Secret Shape Garden

Look at the picture and identify the shapes. Count and write the correct number.

Circles	
Triangles	
Rectangles	
Squares	

Geoboard

A geoboard, also called a pegboard, is a board with nails in a particular pattern.

It is used to explore shapes and their characteristics.

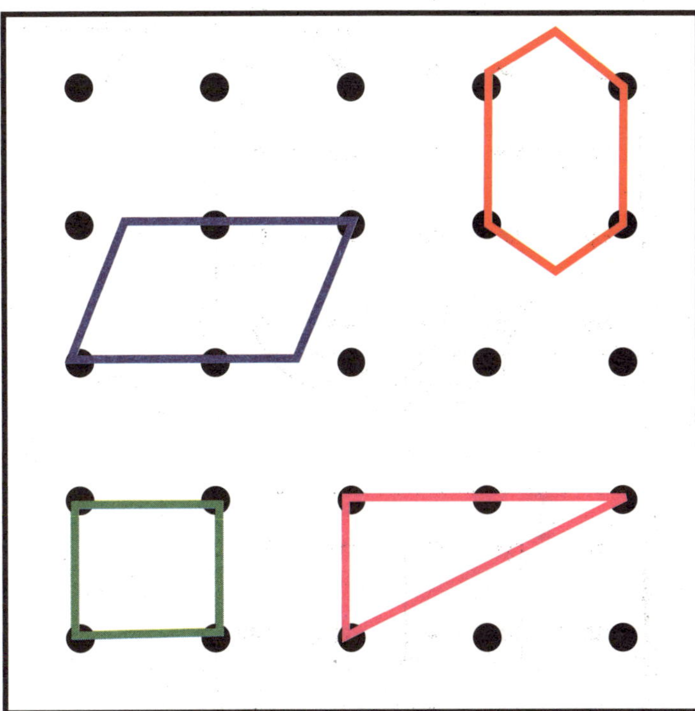

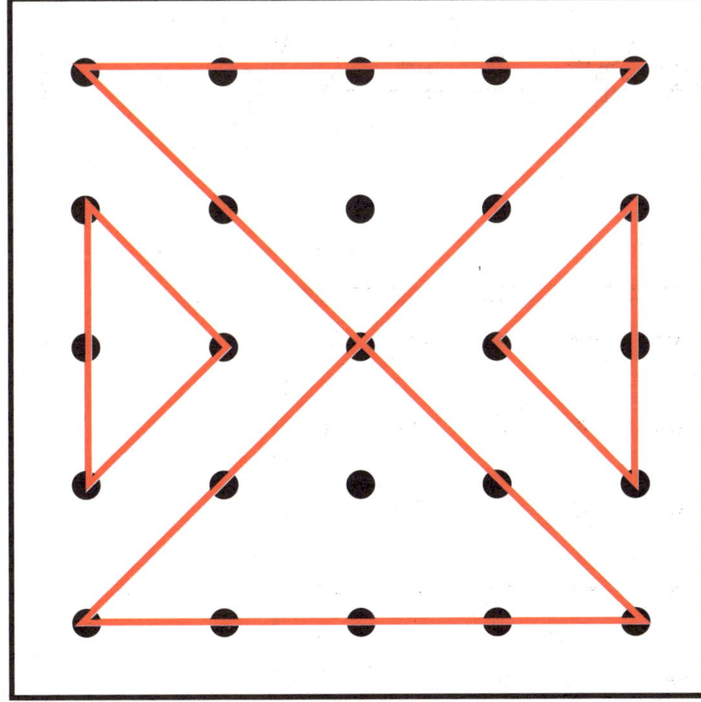

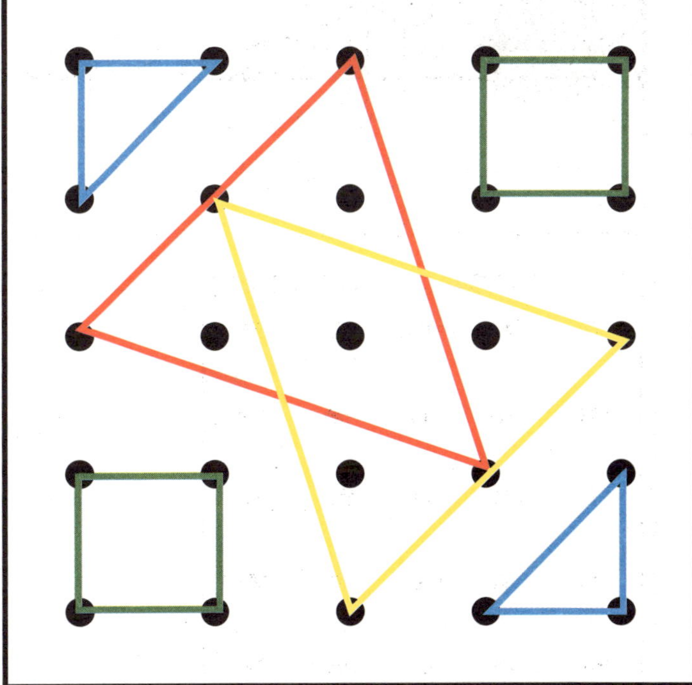

Geoboard

Follow the instructions to make shapes on the geoboards.

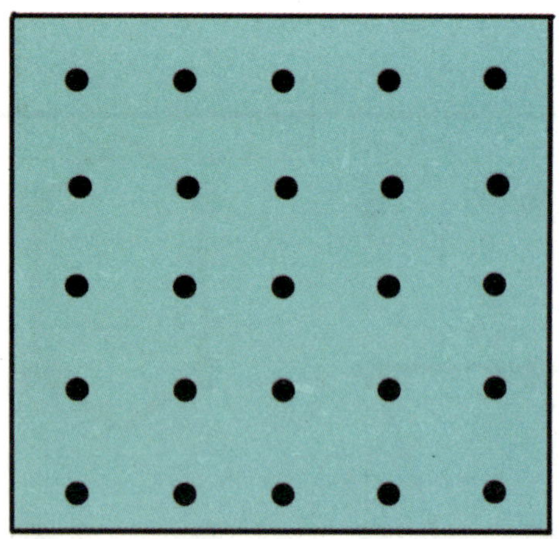

Make a shape with 3 sides.

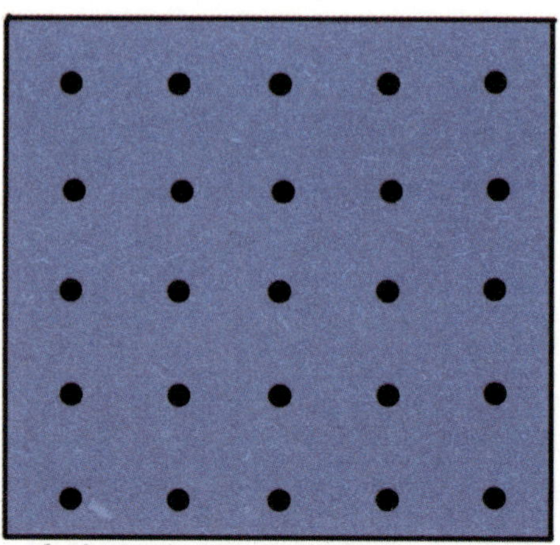

Make a shape with 4 corners.

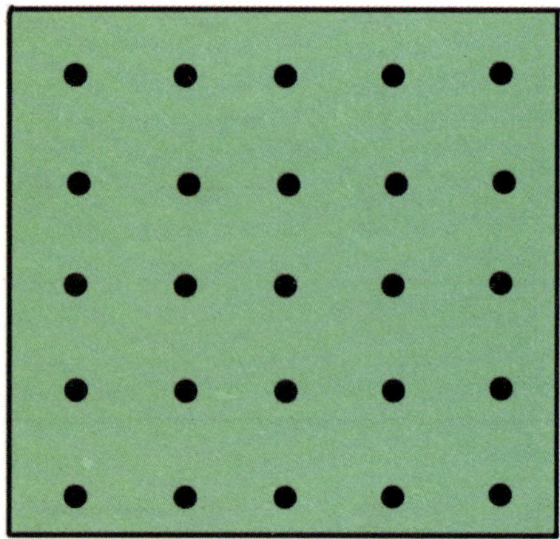

Make a shape with 4 sides that are all equal.

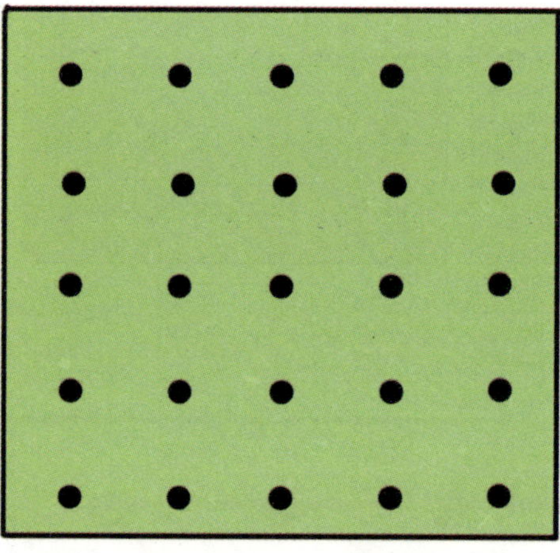

Make a shape with 4 sides, with opposite sides equal.

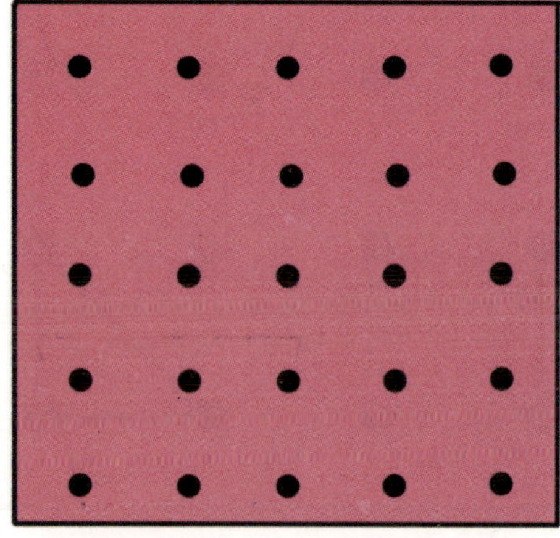

Make a trapezoid.

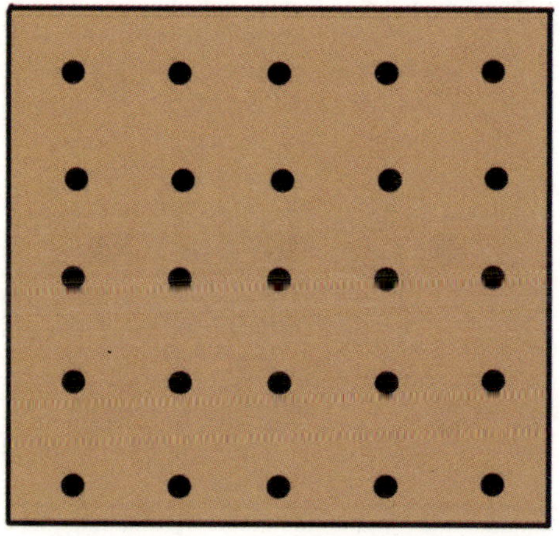

Make a diamond.

Putting Shapes Together

Choose the shapes from the box. Put together two identical shapes. Draw and write about the new shape you made from the two shapes.

1\.

I put together two squares to make a rectangle. It has 4 sides and 4 corners.

2\.

3\.

4\.

5\.

Shape Composition

What shapes are these pictures made of? Draw different shapes in the space on the right. One has been done for you.

3-D Shapes

3-D shapes are fat, not flat.

They have faces, edges and vertices intact.

A **cone** is like a party hat,

A **sphere** is like a bouncy ball.

A **prism** is like a building tall!

A **cylinder** is like a can you pop.

A **cube** is like the dice you drop.

3-D shapes are here and there,

You can see 3-D shapes everywhere!

A 3-D shape is a solid figure that is 3 dimensional and has length, width and depth.

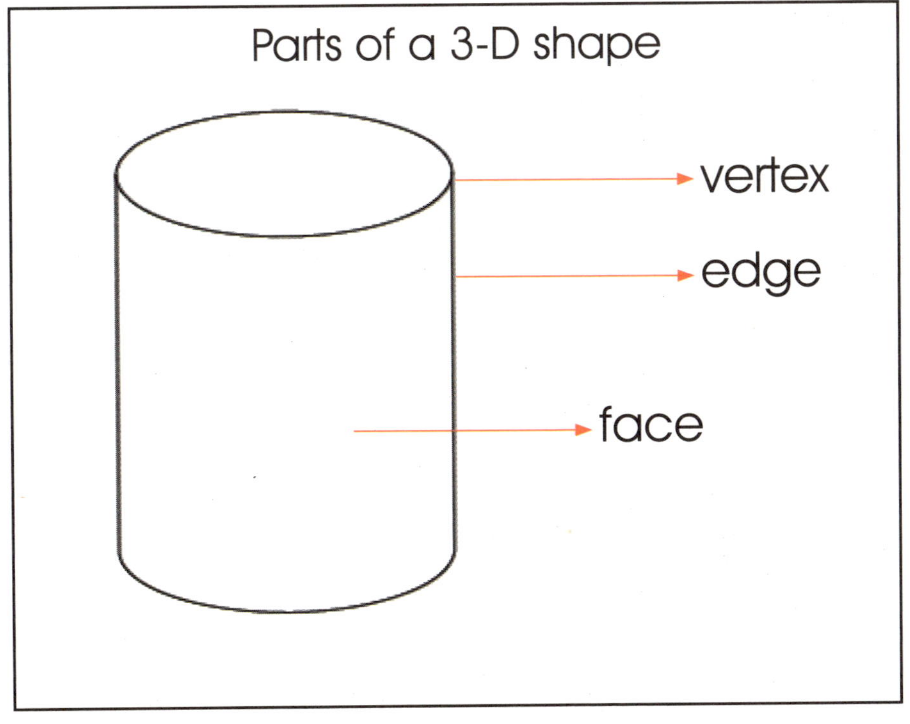

Cone

A cone has:

1 face

1 vertex

no edges

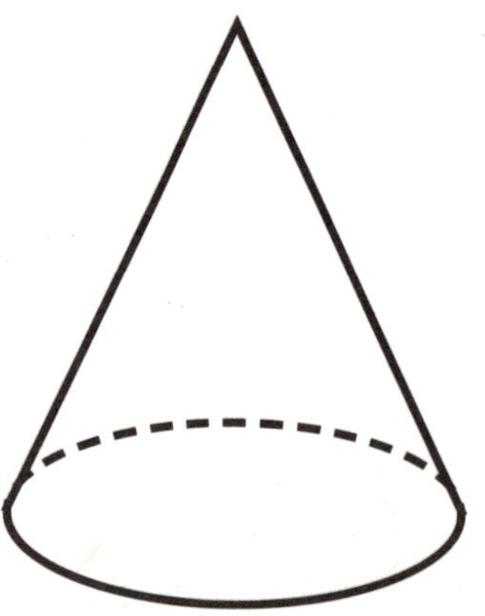

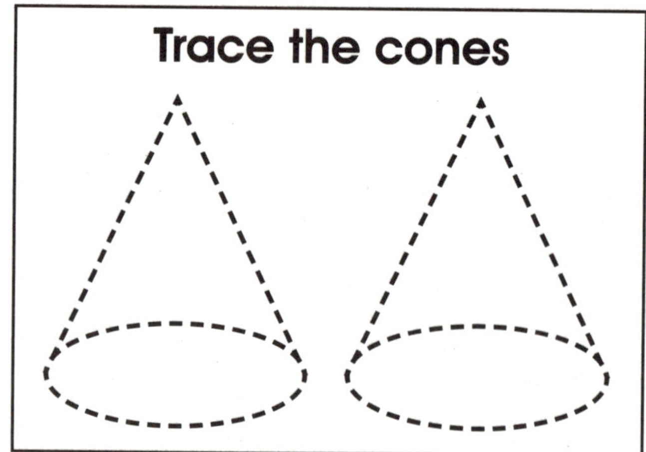

Tick the objects that are conical in shape.

Does a cone...

- Roll? ____________________
- Stack? ____________________
- Slide? ____________________

Draw a cone

Cylinder

A cylinder has:

2 faces

no vertex

no edges

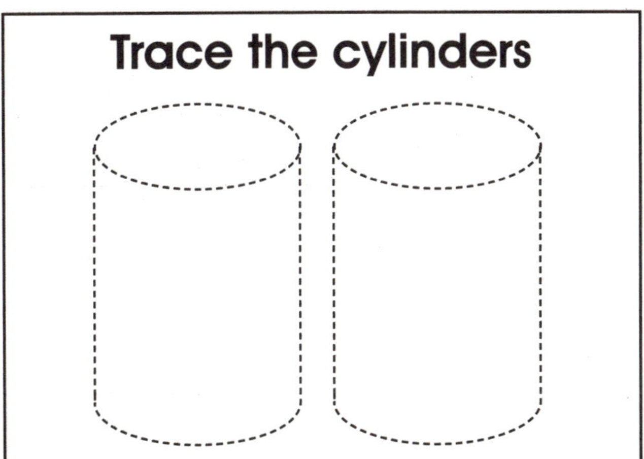

Circle the objects that are cylinder-shaped.

Does a cylinder...

- Roll? ______________
- Stack? ______________
- Slide? ______________

Draw a cylinder

Cube

A cube has:

6 faces

8 vertices

12 edges

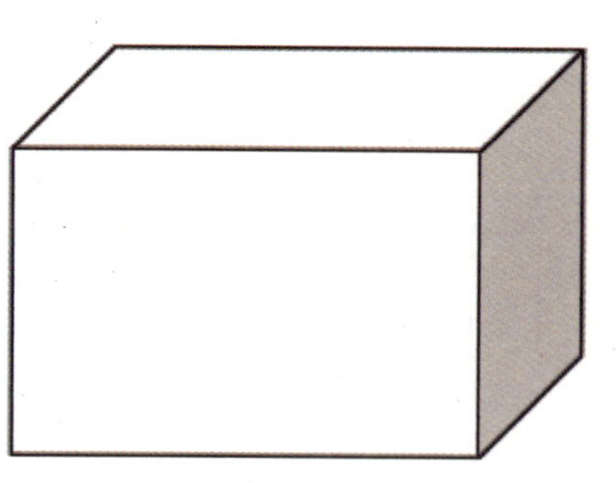

Trace the cubes

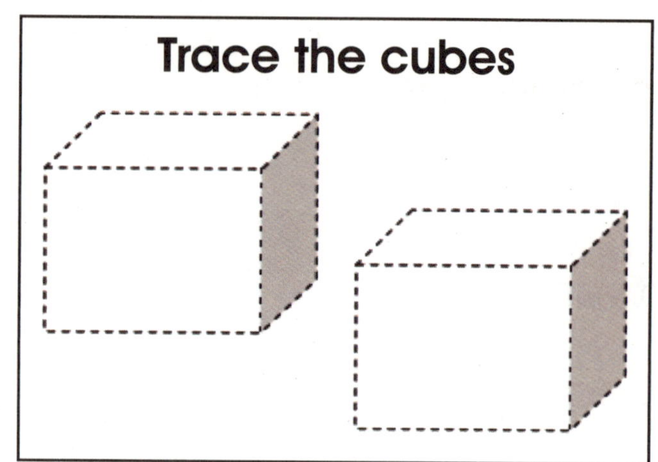

Circle the objects that are cubes in shape.

Does a cube...

- Roll? ____________
- Stack? ____________
- Slide? ____________

Draw a cube

Rectangular Prism

A rectangular prism has:

6 faces

8 vertices

12 edges

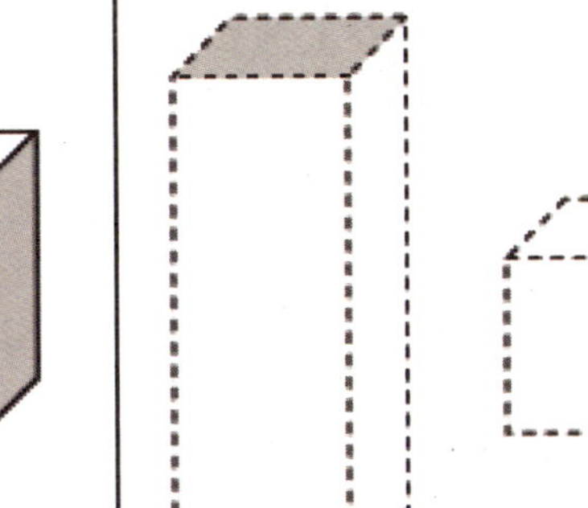

Trace the rectangular prism

Tick the objects that have the shape of a rectangular prism.

Does a rectangular prism...

- Roll? ____________________
- Stack? ____________________
- Slide? ____________________

Draw a rectangular prism

Pyramid

A pyramid has:

5 faces

5 vertices

8 edges

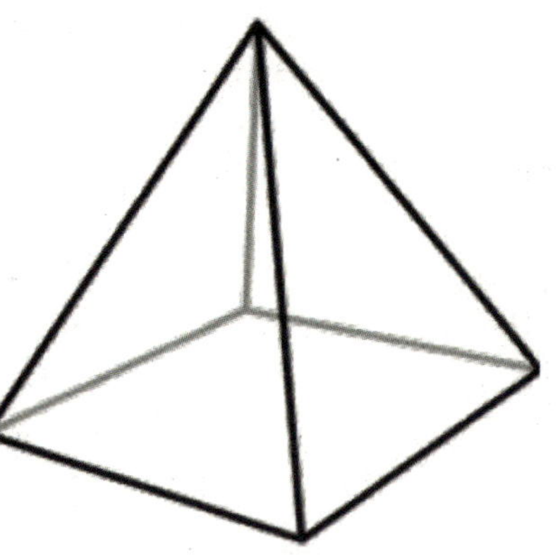

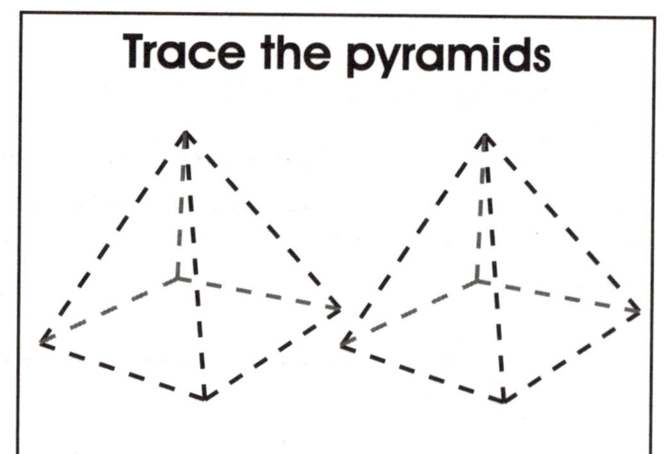

Circle the objects that are pyramid-shaped.

Does a pyramid...

- Roll? ____________
- Stack? ____________
- Slide? ____________

Draw a pyramid

Sphere

A sphere has:

no faces

no vertices

no edges

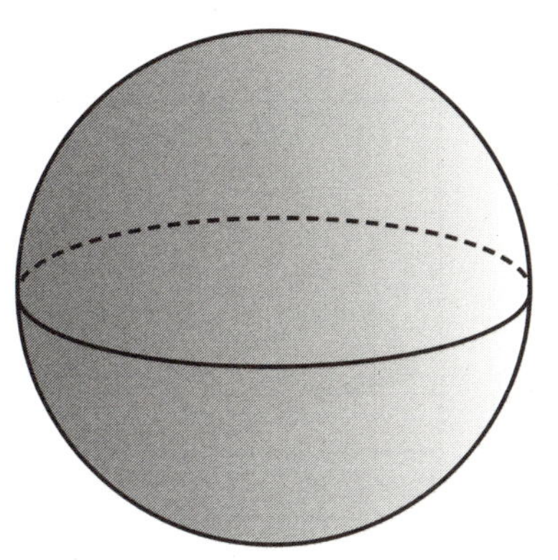

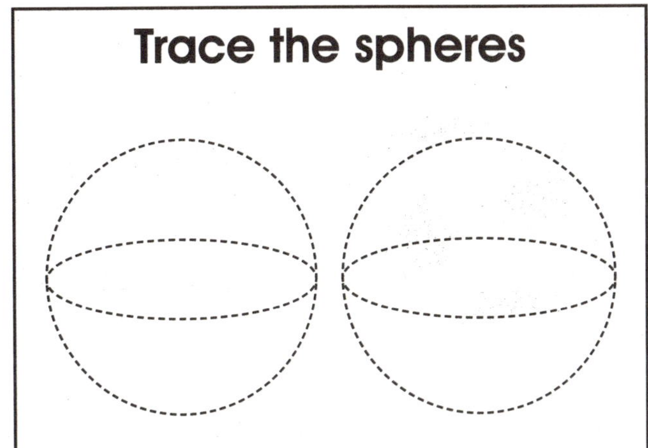

Tick the objects that are spherical in shape.

Does a sphere...

- Roll? ____________
- Stack? ____________
- Slide? ____________

Draw a sphere

More on 3-D Shapes

Match the shapes to their names.

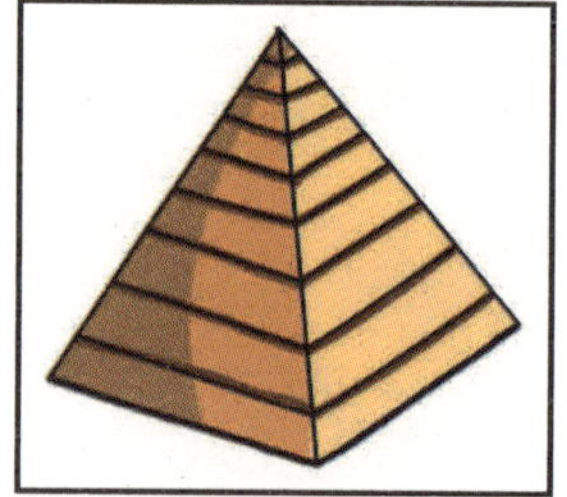
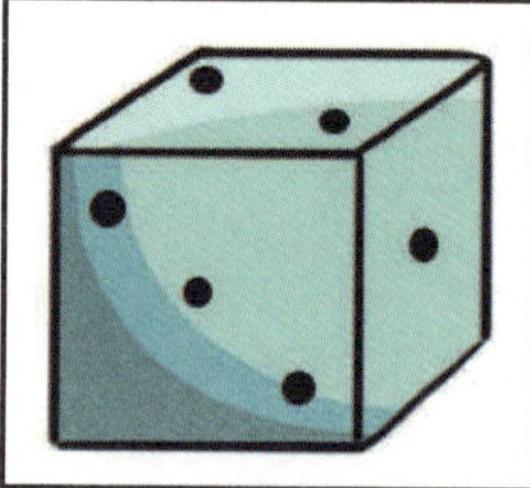

pyramid	sphere	cube	rectangular prism

Count the number of shapes and write the number.

Count and write how many.

Matching 2-D and 3-D Shapes

Draw a line to connect the 3-D shapes with their 2-D look alikes.

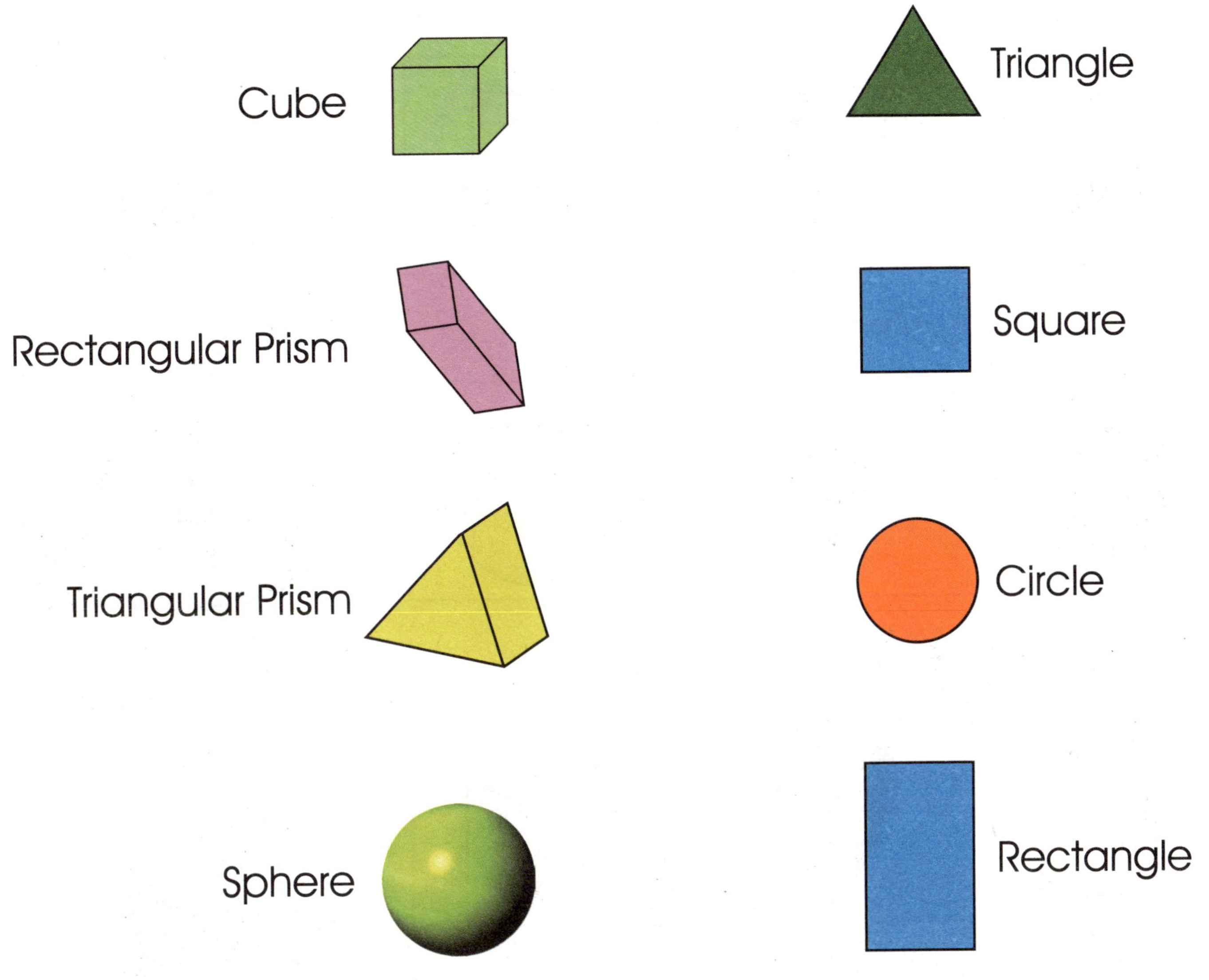

Draw a picture of your own using 3-D shapes.

Roll, Slide or Stack?

1. Tick the objects that roll.

2. Circle the objects that slide.

3. Tick the objects that stack.

4. Cross the objects that roll and slide.

5. Circle the objects that slide and stack.

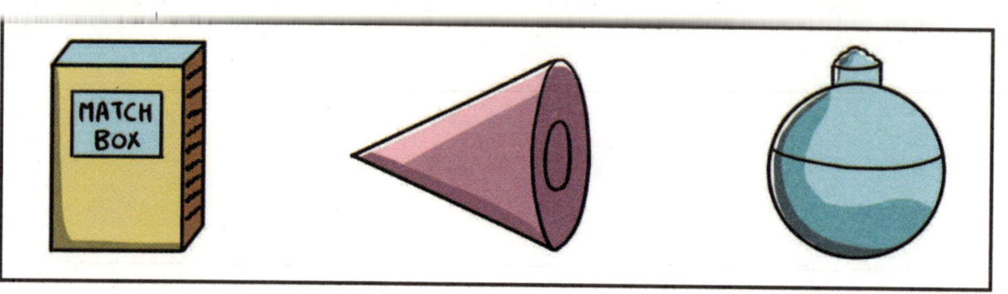

A 3-D shape may:

Equal Parts of a Shape

We can divide shapes into equal parts. These are whole shapes.

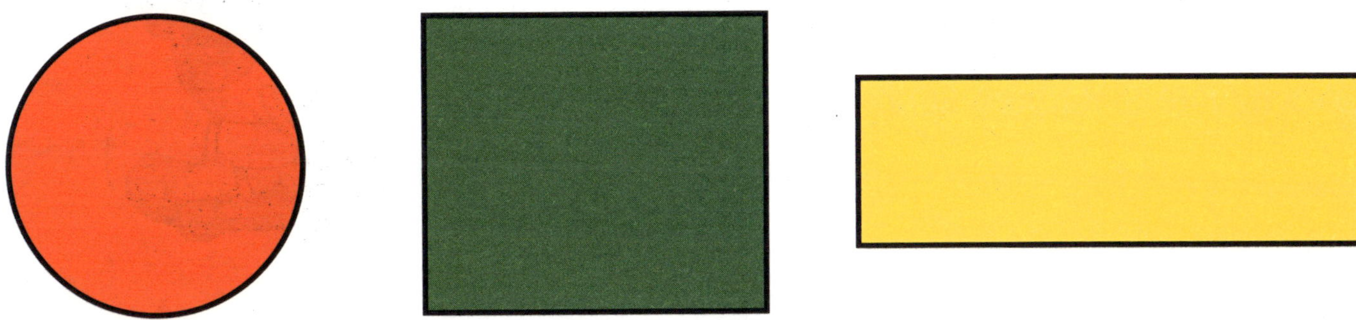

We can divide shapes into two equal parts. These parts are called **halves.**

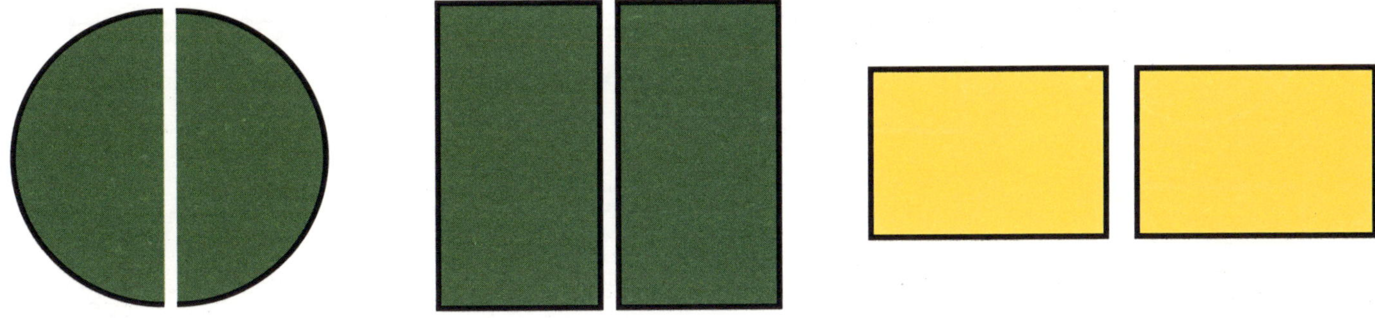

We can divide shapes into four equal parts. These parts are called **quarters** or **fourths.**

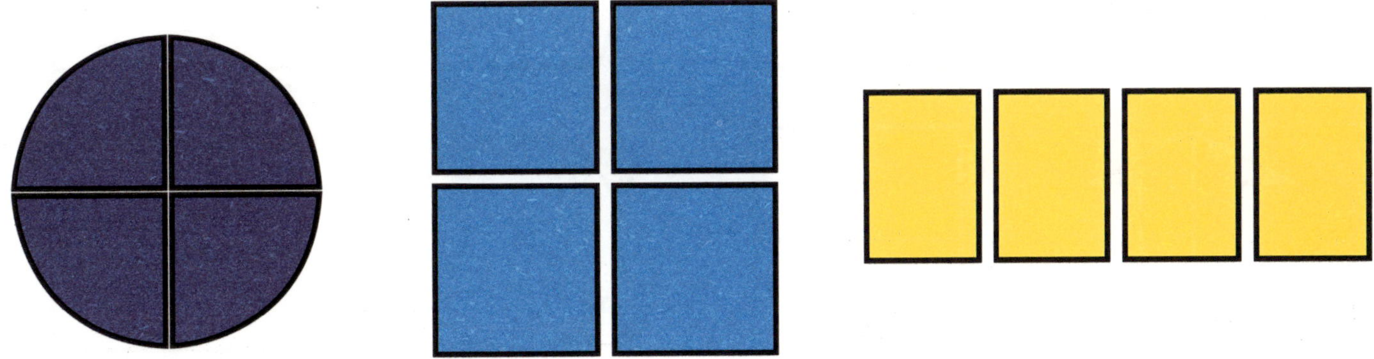

Colouring Equal Parts

Colour the shapes showing 1 whole RED.

Colour the shapes split into halves GREEN.

Colour the shapes split into quarters BLUE.

Dividing shapes into equal parts

Draw a line to divide these shapes into halves.

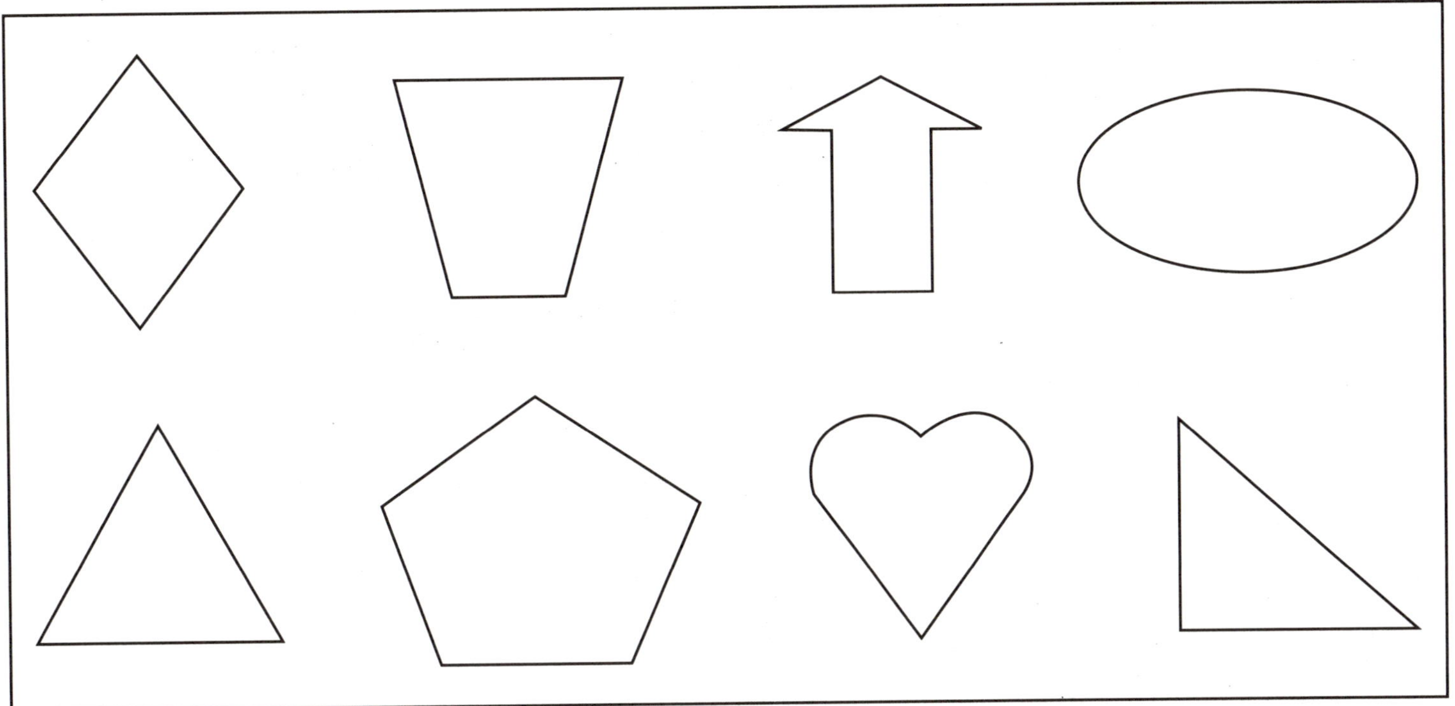

Draw a line to divide these shapes into fourths.

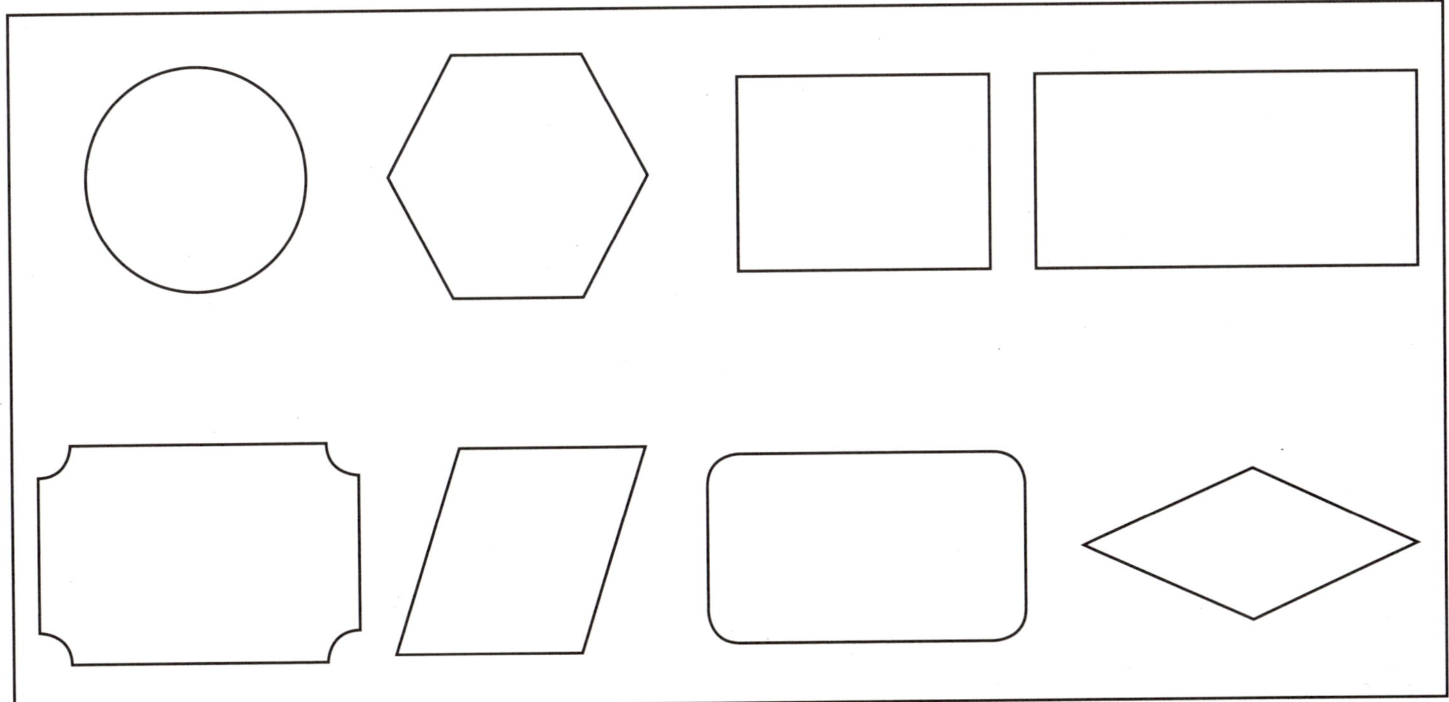

ANSWER KEY

Page 2

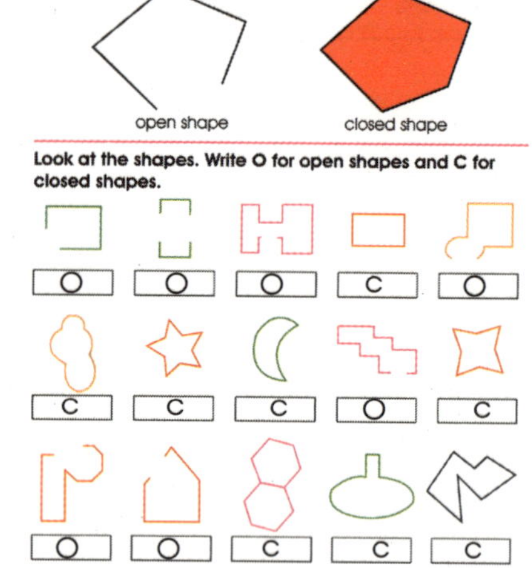

Page 3

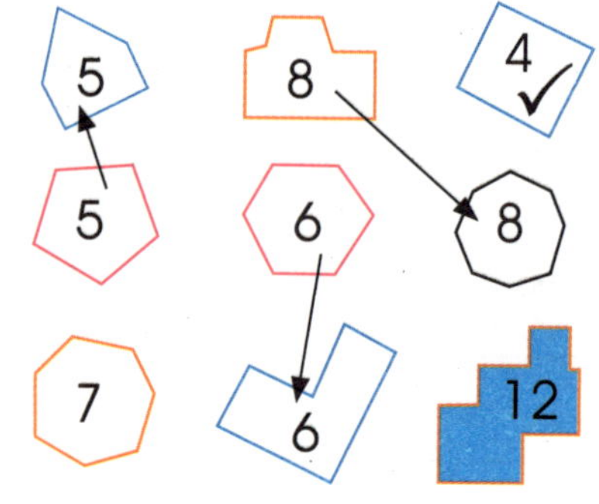

Page 4

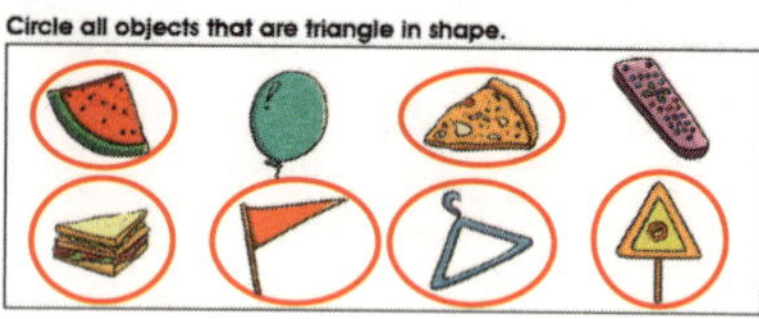

Page 5

Page 6

Page 7

Page 8

Page 9

Page 10

The shapes are:

1. rectangle
2. triangle
3. oval
4. square
5. circle
6. cone
7. trapezoid

Children will draw shapes on their own.

Page 11

Children will do on their own.

Page 12

Circles: 15

Triangles: 10

Rectangles: 6

Squares: 1

Page 14

Children will do on their own.

Page 15

Children will do on their own.

ANSWER KEY

Page 16

Page 18

Page 19

Page 20

Page 21

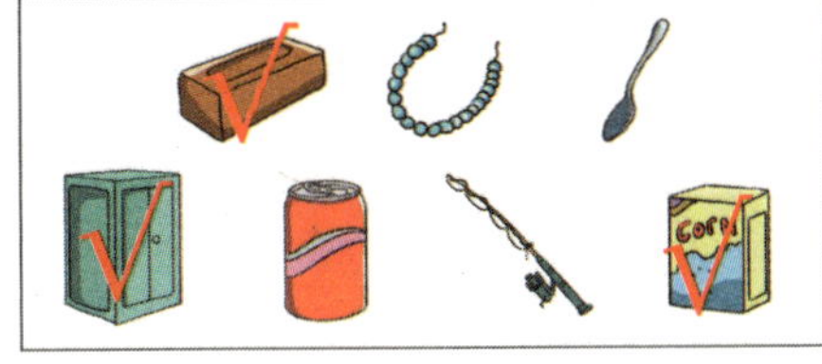

Page 22

Page 23

Page 24

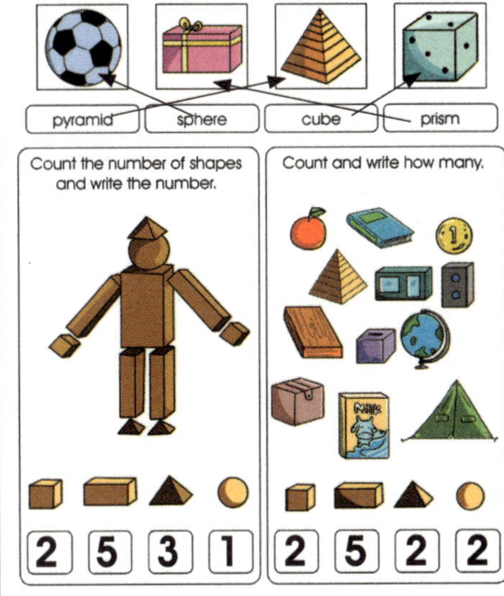

Page 25

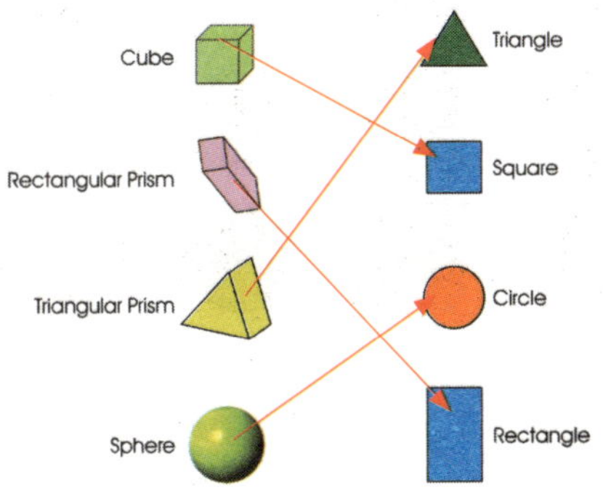

ANSWER KEY

Page 26

Page 28

Page 29

Children will do on their own.